IS-253.A: Overview of FEMA's Environmental and Historic Preservation Review

By

Fema

10/31/2013

Lesson 1: Introduction and Course Overview

Course Welcome

Welcome to the Overview of FEMA Environmental and Historic Preservation (EHP) course.

This course is designed to help you understand FEMA's environmental and historic preservation compliance responsibilities. This course will:

- Introduce EHP compliance requirements.
- Present EHP requirements as they relate to FEMA's mission, programs, and activities.

Key Course Themes

This course is built around three key themes.

- Identifying the roles and responsibilites of all stakeholders
- The importance of accurate information and complete project descriptions
- Identifying opportunites to streamline the EHP review process

Course Objectives

At the end of this course, you should be able to:

- Describe the basic elements of Federal EHP laws, regulations, and Executive Orders.
- Describe key roles and responsibilities in the EHP process.
- Identify activities that trigger EHP review.
- Explain the consequences of non-compliance with EHP requirements.

The lessons in this course and a description of their content are shown in the table below.

Lesson	Description
1. Introduction and Course Overview	This lesson describes procedures for completing this course and presents the course goal, objectives, and topics to be covered.
2. The National Environmental Policy Act	This lesson presents the basic requirements of the National Environmental Policy Act (NEPA). It includes FEMA's EHP responsibilities under NEPA, the levels of NEPA review, and elements of a good scope of work.
3. Other Environmental Laws	This lesson introduces environmental laws and regulations typically encountered on FEMA-funded projects. It will describe FEMA's responsibilities under various biological, coastal, water resource, pollution control, debris management, and socioeconomic laws; identify FEMA actions that trigger review under certain environmental laws; and outline applicant and sub-applicant roles and responsibilities for compliance with environmental laws, Executive Orders (EOs), and regulations.
4. The National Historic Preservation Act	This lesson describes FEMA's responsibilities under the National Historic Preservation Act (NHPA), including identifying FEMA actions that trigger historic preservation review, the characteristics of potential historic properties, identifying potential adverse effects to identified properties and resolving those effects, and methods to expedite FEMA's historic preservation review process.
5. Course Summary	This lesson provides a summary of the key points in this course to prepare you for the final exam.

Lesson Objectives

At the end of this lesson you should be able to:

- Navigate through this course.
- Describe the topics and content of this course.
- List the preparedness mission areas and provide an example of each.
- Explain how EHP supports FEMA's overall mission.
- Discuss the legal foundation for EHP compliance.

FEMA's Mission

The Robert T. Stafford Disaster Relief and Emergency Assistance Act, as amended (The Stafford Act), provides the national foundation for emergency and disaster response, recovery, and mitigation. Unless otherwise assigned by the President, FEMA acts as the lead agency for these actions.

FEMA's mission was developed based on The Stafford Act.

"FEMA's mission is to support our citizens and first responders to ensure that as a nation we work together to build, sustain, and improve our capability to prepare for, protect against, respond to, recovery from, and mitigate all hazards."

Presidential Preparedness Directive 8 (PPD-8)

Presidential Preparedness Directive 8 (PPD-8) establishes a vision for the whole community–including individuals, businesses, community- and faith-based organizations; schools; tribes; and all levels of government—to work together to develop a:

- National Preparedness Goal.
- National Preparedness System Description.
- Series of National Frameworks and Federal Interagency Operational Plans.
- National Preparedness Report.
- Campaign To Build and Sustain Preparedness.

The National Preparedness Goal

The National Preparedness Goal (NPG) presents an integrated, layered, and all-of-Nation approach to preparedness.

Successful achievement of this goal will result in a secure and resilient Nation with the **capabilities** required across the whole community to prevent, protect against, mitigate, respond to, and recover from the threats and hazards that pose the greatest risk.

FEMA's areas of emphasis remain in the mitigation, response, and recovery mission areas.

National Preparedness Goal: Capabilities and Mission Areas

The emphasis of the National Preparedness Goal is on building and sustaining core capabilities across five mission areas.

Mission Areas

Mission areas differ from phases of emergency management. Each area is comprised of the capabilities required for achieving the mission or function at any time (before, during, or after an incident) and across all threats and hazards. **It is important to shift your thinking to capabilities!**

Prevention: The capabilities necessary to avoid, prevent, or stop a threatened or actual act of **terrorism**. As defined by PPD-8, the term "prevention" refers to **preventing imminent threats**.

Protection: The capabilities necessary to secure the homeland against acts of **terrorism and manmade or natural disasters**.

Mitigation: The capabilities necessary to **reduce loss of life and property by lessening the impact of disasters**.

Response: The capabilities necessary to **save lives, protect property and the environment, and meet basic human needs** after an incident has occurred.

Recovery: The capabilities necessary to assist communities affected by an incident to **recover effectively**.

Core Capabilities

Core capabilities are:

- Distinct critical elements necessary to meet the National Preparedness Goal.
- Essential for the execution of each mission area: Prevention, Protection, Mitigation, Response, and Recovery.

EHP's Core Capability

EHP's core capability is in the Recovery Mission Area: **Natural and Cultural Resources**

Protect natural and cultural resources and historic properties through appropriate planning, mitigation, response, and recovery actions to preserve, conserve, rehabilitate, and restore them consistent with post-disaster community priorities and best practices and in compliance with appropriate environmental and historic preservation laws, implementing regulations, and executive orders.

FEMA's Mission and EHP

EHP integrates the protection and enhancement of environmental, historic, and cultural resources into FEMA's mission, programs, and activities by:

- Ensuring FEMA actions comply with Federal EHP laws and Executive Orders.
- Incorporating EHP values into all of FEMA's programs and activities.

FEMA's EHP review and compliance activities should be initiated early in the project life cycle and not be treated as a separate process.

FEMA's Legal Responsibility

All Federal projects must comply with the relevant EHP laws.

Regardless of timing or funding program, these types of FEMA activities generally have a higher potential to impact EHP resources.

- New construction requiring ground disturbance.

- Modification, expansion, or mitigation of existing facilities.
- Work in or around water.
- Debris removal and disposal.
- Demolition.

Sources of FEMA's Authority

FEMA gains its authority through several sources.

Laws:
Enacted by Congress and signed by the President, laws provide the legal basis and funding for programs and/or projects. Observance of Federal, State, local and Tribal laws is obligatory. Example: The Stafford Act (P.L. 93-288, as amended)

Executive Orders:
Issued by the President to Federal agencies, EOs have the force and effect of law. Example: EO 11990, Protection of Wetlands

Regulations:
Rules that implement laws and regulations are based on the interpretation of law. Regulations must be within the agency's statutory authority as proscribed in the agency's enabling legislation. After public vetting, regulations have the force of law. Example: 44 Code of Federal Regulations (CFR), Federal Management and Assistance

Policies:
Rules issued to clarify laws and regulations as they relate to specific agency actions. Example: PAA 9500

FEMA's Statutory Authorities: The Stafford Act

FEMA's foundational law is the Robert T. Stafford Disaster Relief and Emergency Assistance Act (P.L. 93-288), as amended. The Stafford Act constitutes the statutory authority for most Federal disaster response and recovery activities.

FEMA has additional authorities under:

- National Flood Insurance Act
- Disaster Mitigation Act of 2000
- Post-Katrina Emergency Management Reform Act

Consequences of Non-Compliance

Failure to comply with processes and procedures as outlined in applicable laws and Executive Orders could result in:

- Delay in or loss of funding.
- Adverse publicity.
- Criminal or civil penalties.

Lesson Summary

You have now completed Lesson 1 of the course. You should be able to:

- Describe the topics and content of this course.
- List the preparedness mission areas and provide an example of each.
- Explain how EHP supports FEMA's overall mission.
- Discuss the legal foundation for EHP compliance.

Lesson 2 will describe the National Environmental Policy Act (NEPA).

Lesson 2: The National Environmental Policy Act

Lesson Overview

This lesson introduces the main components of the National Environmental Policy Act (NEPA).

At the end of this lesson, you should be able to:

- Describe FEMA's EHP responsibilities under NEPA.
- Identify elements of a good scope of work.
- Describe levels of NEPA review.

National Environmental Policy Act

The National Environmental Policy Act (NEPA) provides the basis for the establishment of a national environmental strategy. The primary goals of NEPA are to:

- Obligate Federal agencies to consider the potential impacts of their actions to the human environment (physical, natural, cultural and social) before proceeding.
- Require consideration of alternatives to the proposed action.
- Ensure that the agency will provide an opportunity for public input into the decisionmaking process.

NEPA Scope

Any amount of Federal funding spent on a project requires compliance with NEPA, regardless of the total project cost. While all FEMA grants (disaster and non-disaster) are considered Federal projects, some FEMA funded projects are statutorily exempt from NEPA review.
NEPA requires a decisionmaking process and documentation, not a specific outcome.

Agencies may decide that other values (socio-economic concerns, cost effectiveness or technical feasibility) may outweigh the environmental impacts.

What is FEMA's NEPA Responsibility?

NEPA requires FEMA to:

- Define the action.
- Determine the level of NEPA review required.
- Collect information about the environmental resources that may be present in the area of an action.
- Determine and evaluate the effects of the proposed action and alternatives.
- Ensure that project information is available to the public.

An incomplete or inaccurate scope of work can delay the NEPA review process and expose FEMA to legal challenges.

NEPA compliance is not a substitute for complying with other environmental and historic preservation (EHP) laws and executive orders (EOs).

Defining a Good Scope of Work

A good scope of work (SOW) will have different elements based on the type of project it is; however, at a minimum it should include:

- Project location, including street address or closest crossing streets of the project site and latitude and longitude, in decimal degrees.
- A narrative description of the actions to be taken.
- The dimensions and quantities of materials proposed for the project.
- Any needed graphics (maps, photos, sketches, plans, etc.).
- Proposed dates of construction of all structures in the project area.
- A description of all actions related to the project, even if not being funded by FEMA.

The scope of eligible work for disaster and non-disaster FEMA-funded projects must:

- Be clear, concise, and accurate, and use quantifiable and descriptive terms.
- Include the proposed project location (including staging areas and construction access), site plans, required permits, color photographs, etc.
- Provide clear understanding of key project components and distinguish between work that has been completed and work that remains.

It is important to provide complete and accurate information to facilitate EHP review and avoid unnecessary delays.

The work should be specified as an action with quantifiable (e.g., length, width, depth, or capacity) and descriptive (e.g., brick, wood, asphalt, timber, or deck bridge) terms. The scope of work should not be described only as "restore to pre-disaster design." If part of the work is completed prior to project approval, the work that has been completed should be distinguished from work remaining.

Any other information that is pertinent to the scope of work should be documented.
Examples include:

- Eligible codes and standards. Copies of specific codes and standards should be included, especially if a proposed project exceeds the pre-disaster design.
- Evidence of pre-disaster damage, such as cracks on a steel bridge covered by rust and corrosion.
- Pre-disaster inspection reports, noting deficiencies.
- A description of ineligible work, maintenance, inactive facilities, and/or responsibilities of other Federal agencies.
- Reference to a hazard mitigation proposal, if one is included for the project.
- A complete description of the overall project.
- Proposed special equipment or construction approach, such as heavy trucks, access roads, staging area, coffer dams, etc.
- A description of the larger action, if the action is part of one (e.g., one building in a complex).

Example: Damage Description and Dimensions:

Floodwaters from Fern Creek overtopped Fernwood Drive, a 26-foot wide roadway with 3-inch asphalt pavement and 8-inch aggregate base, located in the Village of Bolingbrook. The floodwaters washed out a 150-linear-foot (LF) by 26-LF section of the roadway pavement and aggregate base. Additionally, the fill embankment—26-foot wide (top) x 4-foot high x 42-foot wide (bottom)—was washed out for a length of 100 LF beneath the damaged section of roadway. Floodwaters damaged 300 LF of steel guardrail (150 LF on each side) along the entire stretch of the washed-out road.

Scope of Work:

Replace fill embankment with unclassified fill for 100-LF x 4-feet (high) x 26-feet (top width) x 42-feet (bottom width). Replace 150-LF x 26-feet x
8-inch base course and 150 LF x 26-feet x 3-inch asphalt pavement. Remove and replace 300 LF of steel guardrail. Place 100 LF of 1-foot thick x 2-foot high riprap along the stream side of the constructed embankment slope in accordance with the Village of Bolingbrook Code Provision #101A (attached).

NEPA Levels of Review

Based on the SOW, there are four possible outcomes or levels of review: The level of review is determined by the number and extent of environmental impacts.

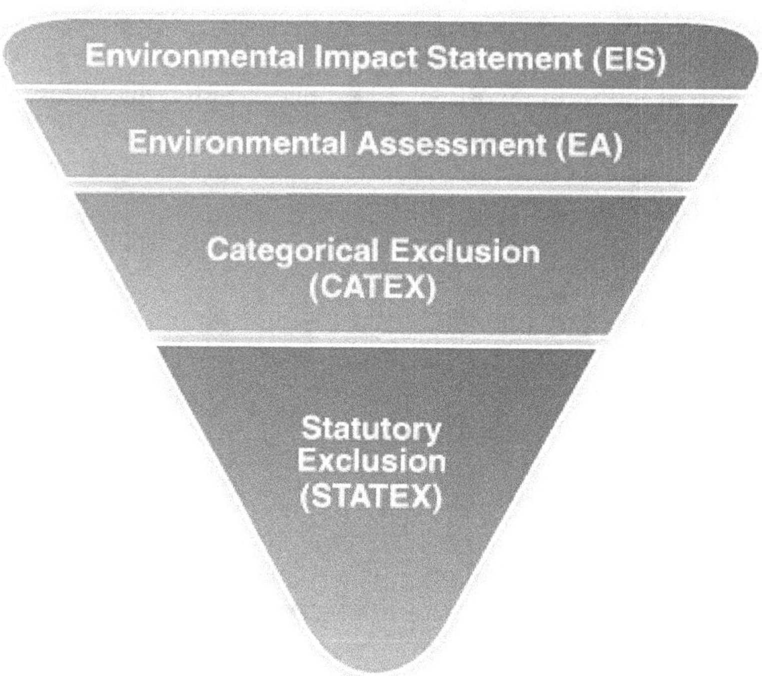

NEPA Levels of Review: Environmental Impact Statement

NEPA requires an Environmental Impact Statement (EIS) for all Federal actions significantly affecting the quality of the human environment. EISs:

- Are the highest level of NEPA review.
- Include an in-depth analysis of large-scale, complex Federal actions.
- May take years to complete.
- Are expensive to produce.
- Are rarely required by FEMA actions.
- Require extensive public involvement.

NEPA Level of Review: Environmental Assessment

The Environmental Assessment (EA) is also a document that describes and evaluates potential impacts of an action on the human environment and is used to determine if an EIS will be required.

- Second highest level of NEPA review
- Concise analysis of federal actions where the environmental impacts are uncertain
- May take months to complete
- Must include some level of public notification
- Typically required by FEMA actions that involve significant modifications or new construction

Typical Actions that require an EA are shown below.

- New construction projects
- Temporary housing on undeveloped sites
- Relocating facilities
- Large-scale drainage projects
- Controversial actions

EAs must include:

- A description of the purpose and need of the project.
- A description of the proposed action and alternatives considered.
- Identified impacts of the proposed action and alternatives.
- A record of consultation and coordination.
- Opportunities for public involvement.

An Environmental Assessment has two possible outcomes.

- Finding of No Significant Impact (FONSI) states the action will have no significant effect to the human environment. No EIS is required.
- Notice of Intent (NOI) announces an agency's intent to prepare an EIS because significant impacts are possible.

NEPA Level of Review: Categorical Exclusion

Categorical Exclusions (CATEXs) are exemptions for specific types of actions determined to have no significant impacts on human environment. CATEXs:

- Are the third highest level of NEPA review.
- Streamline the NEPA process.

- Can be completed in much shorter timeframe than an EA or EIS.
- Do not require an analysis of alternatives.
- Satisfy public notice requirements when established.

FEMA currently has 19 CATEXs, which are found in 44 CFR Part 10.8 (d).

CATEX

i. Administrative actions, such as personnel actions, travel, procurement of supplies, etc., in support of normal day-to-day activities and disaster-related activities

ii. Preparation, revision, and adoption of regulations, directives, manuals, and other guidance documents related to actions that qualify for categorical exclusions

iii. Studies that involve no commitment of resources other than manpower and associated funding

iv. Inspection and monitoring activities, granting of variances, and actions to enforce Federal, State, or local codes, standards, or regulations

v. Training activities and both training and operational exercises utilizing existing facilities in accordance with established procedures and land use designations

vi. Procurement of goods and services for support of day-to-day and emergency operational activities, and the temporary storage of goods other than hazardous materials, so long as storage occurs on previously disturbed land or in existing facilities

vii. The acquisition of properties and the associated demolition/removal [see paragraph (d)(2)(xii) of this section] or relocation of structures [see paragraph (d)(2)(xiii) of this section] under any applicable authority when the acquisition is from a willing seller, the buyer coordinated acquisition planning with affected authorities, and the acquired property will be dedicated in perpetuity to uses that are compatible with open space, recreational, or wetland practices

viii. Acquisition or lease of existing facilities where planned uses conform to past use or local land use requirements

ix. Acquisition, installation, or operation of utility and communication systems that use existing distribution systems or facilities, or currently used infrastructure rights-of-way

x. Routine maintenance, repair, and groundskeeping activities at FEMA facilities

xi. Planting of indigenous vegetation

xii. Demolition of structures and other improvements, or disposal of uncontaminated structures and other improvements to permitted offsite locations, or both

xiii. Physical relocation of individual structures where FEMA has no involvement in the relocation site selection or development

xiv. Granting of community-wide exceptions for floodproofed residential basements meeting the requirements of 44 CFR 60.6(c) under the National Flood Insurance Program

xv. Repair, reconstruction, restoration, elevation, retrofitting, upgrading to current codes and standards, or replacement of any facility in a manner that substantially conforms to the preexisting design, function, and location

xvi. Improvements to existing facilities and the construction of small-scale hazard mitigation measures in existing developed areas with substantially completed infrastructure, when the immediate project area has already been disturbed, and when those actions do not alter basic functions, do not exceed capacity of other system components, or modify intended land use; provided the operation of the completed project will not, of itself, have an adverse effect on the quality of the human environment

xvii. Actions conducted within enclosed facilities where all airborne emissions, waterborne effluent, external radiation levels, outdoor noise, and solid and bulk waste disposal practices comply with existing Federal, State, and local laws and regulations

xviii. The following planning and administrative activities in support of emergency and disaster response and recovery:

    A. Activation of the Emergency Support Team and convening of the Catastrophic Disaster Response Group at FEMA headquarters;

    B. Activation of the Regional Operations Center and deployment of the Emergency Response Team, in whole or in part;

    C. Deployment of Urban Search and Rescue teams;

    D. Situation Assessment including ground and aerial reconnaissance;

    E. Information and data gathering and reporting efforts in support of emergency and disaster response and recovery and hazard mitigation; and

xix. The following emergency and disaster response, recovery and hazard mitigation activities under the Stafford Act:

    A. General Federal Assistance (Sec. 402); [SE]

    B. Essential Assistance (Sec. 403); [SE]

    C. Debris Removal (Sec. 407) [SE]

    D. Temporary Housing (Sec. 408), except locating multiple mobile homes or other readily fabricated dwellings on sites, other than private residences, not previously used for such purposes;

    E. Unemployment Assistance (Sec. 410);

    F. Individual and Family Grant Programs (Sec. 411), except for grants that will be used for restoring, repairing or building private bridges, or purchasing mobile homes or other readily fabricated dwellings;

    G. Food Coupons and Distribution (Sec. 412);

    H. Food Commodities (Sec. 413);

    I. Legal Services (Sec. 415);

    J. Crisis Counseling Assistance and Training (Sec. 416);

K. Community Disaster Loans (Sec. 417);
L. Emergency Communications (Sec. 418);
M. Emergency Public Transportation (Sec. 419);
N. Fire Suppression Grants (Sec. 420); and
O. Federal Emergency Assistance (Sec. 502) [SE].

If extraordinary circumstances are present, a normally CATEX-able action may be elevated to an Environmental Assessment.

i. Greater scope or size than normally experienced for a particular category of action
ii. Actions with a high level of public controversy
iii. Potential for degradation, even though slight, of already existing poor environmental conditions
iv. Employment of unproven technology with potential adverse effects or actions involving unique or unknown environmental risks
v. Presence of endangered or threatened species or their critical habitat, or archaeological, cultural, historical or other protected resources
vi. Presence of hazardous or toxic substances at levels which exceed Federal, State, or local regulations or standards requiring action or attention
vii. Actions with the potential to affect special status areas adversely, or other critical resources such as wetlands, coastal zones, wildlife refuge and wilderness areas, wild and scenic rivers, or sole or principal drinking water aquifers
viii. Potential for adverse effects on health or safety
ix. Potential to violate a Federal, State, local, or Tribal law or requirements imposed for the protection of the environment
x. Potential for significant cumulative impact when the proposed action is combined with other past, present, and reasonably foreseeable future actions, even though the impacts of the proposed action may not be significant by themselves

NEPA Levels of Review: Statutory Exclusions (STATEX)

Statutory exclusions are exemptions from NEPA review granted by Stafford Act and implemented in 44 CFR, 10.8(c). They exclude projects including those that return facilities to pre-disaster condition.

- FEMA is the only Federal agency with STATEX authority due to its unique disaster mission.
- STATEXs apply only to Public Assistance (PA) and Individual Assistance (IA) projects with little or no impact on the environment.
- STATEXs typically take shortest amount of time to complete and by definition require no review.

- STATEXs comprise the majority of disaster recovery projects.

44 CFR 10.8(c), (excerpt)

44 CFR 10.8(c): Statutory Exclusions

1. The following actions are statutorily excluded from NEPA and the preparation of environmental impact statements and environmental assessments by section 316 of the Robert T. Stafford Disaster Relief and Emergency Assistance Act (Stafford Act), as amended, 42 U.S.C. 5159;
   1. Action taken or assistance provided under sections 402, 403, 407, or 502 of the Stafford Act; and
   2. Action taken or assistance provided under section 406 of the Stafford Act that has the effect of restoring facilities substantially as they existed before a major disaster or emergency.

Stafford Act, Section 316

Protection of environment

An action which is taken or assistance which is provided pursuant to section 5170a, 5170b, 5172, or 5192 of this title, including such assistance provided pursuant to the procedures provided for in section 5189 of this title, which has the effect of restoring a facility substantially to its condition prior to the disaster or emergency, shall not be deemed a major Federal action significantly affecting the quality of the human environment within the meaning of the National Environmental Policy Act of 1969 (83 Stat. 852)
[42 U.S.C. § 4321 et seq.]. Nothing in this section shall alter or affect the applicability of the National Environmental Policy Act of 1969 or other Federal actions taken under this chapter or any other provision of law.

Lesson Summary

You have completed Lesson 2 of the course. You should now be able to describe the:

- Goals of NEPA.
- Elements of a good scope of work.
- Levels of NEPA review.

Lesson 3: Other Environmental Laws

Lesson Overview

This lesson introduces environmental laws and regulations typically encountered on FEMA-funded projects.

At the end of this lesson, you should be able to:

- Describe FEMA's responsibilities under various biological, coastal, water resource, pollution control, debris management, and socioeconomic laws.
- Identify FEMA actions that trigger review under certain environmental laws.
- Outline applicant and sub-applicant roles and responsibilities for compliance with environmental laws, Executive Orders (EOs), and regulations.

Biological Laws

This lesson will cover the following biological laws and how they apply to the FEMA mission:

- Endangered Species Act (ESA)
- Fish and Wildlife Coordination Act (FWCA)
- Migratory Bird Treaty Act (MBTA)
- Bald and Golden Eagle Protection Act (BGEPA)
- Magnuson-Stevens Fishery Conservation and Management Act
- EO 13112, Invasive Species

Endangered Species Act

Enacted in 1973, the Endangered Species Act (ESA):

- Protects endangered and threatened species and their critical habitats.
- Applies to everyone, not just Federal agencies.

There are severe penalties for non-compliance. Projects may be delayed or stopped, and individuals can be prosecuted. Penalties can include fines and/or imprisonment.

Endangered Species Act: Endangered Species

Animals or plants in danger of extinction may be designated as **endangered species.** Some examples of endangered species include the:

- Indiana Bat.
- Pallid Sturgeon.
- Furbish Lousewort.

Endangered Species Act: Threatened Species

Animals or plants that are likely to become endangered may be designated as **threatened species.** Some examples of threatened species include the:

- Gopher Tortoise.
- White-haired Goldenrod.
- Northeastern Beach Tiger Beetle.

Endangered Species Act: Critical Habitat

Specific geographic areas (as defined by legislation) essential for the conservation and management of threatened and endangered species are classified as **critical habitat.**

Endangered Species Act (ESA)

Section 7 of the ESA requires FEMA to consider and determine if its actions have any potential to affect listed species or their critical habitats.

Endangered Species Act: Section 7. INTERAGENCY COOPERATION

    a. FEDERAL AGENCY ACTIONS AND CONSULTATIONS.—
        1. The Secretary shall review other programs administered by him and utilize such programs in furtherance of the purposes of this Act. All other Federal agencies shall, in consultation with and with the assistance of the Secretary, utilize their authorities in furtherance of the purposes of this Act by carrying out programs for the conservation of endangered species and threatened species listed pursuant to section 4 of this Act.

2. Each Federal agency shall, in consultation with and with the assistance of the Secretary, insure that any action authorized, funded, or carried out by such agency (hereinafter in this section referred to as an "agency action") is not likely to jeopardize the continued existence of any endangered species or threatened species or result in the destruction or adverse modification of habitat of such species which is determined by the Secretary, after consultation as appropriate with affected States, to be critical, unless such agency has been granted an exemption for such action by the Committee pursuant to subsection (h) of this section. In fulfilling the requirements of this paragraph each agency shall use the best scientific and commercial data available.

3. Subject to such guidelines as the Secretary may establish, a Federal agency shall consult with the Secretary on any prospective agency action at the request of, and in cooperation with, the prospective permit or license applicant if the applicant has reason to believe that an endangered species or a threatened species may be present in the area affected by his project and that implementation of such action will likely affect such species.

4. Each Federal agency shall confer with the Secretary on any agency action which is likely to jeopardize the continued existence of any species proposed to be listed under section 4 or result in the destruction or adverse modification of critical habitat proposed to be designated for such species. This paragraph does not require a limitation on the commitment of resources as described in subsection (d).

b. OPINION OF SECRETARY.—

1.

A. Consultation under subsection (a)(2) with respect to any agency action shall be concluded within the 90-day period beginning on the date on which initiated or, subject to subparagraph (B), within such other period of time as is mutually agreeable to the Secretary and the Federal agency.

B. In the case of an agency action involving a permit or license applicant, the Secretary and the Federal agency may not mutually agree to conclude consultation within a period exceeding 90 days unless the Secretary, before the close of the 90th day referred to in subparagraph (A)—

 i. if the consultation period proposed to be agreed to will end before the 150th day after the date on which consultation was initiated, submits to the applicant a written statement setting forth—

  I. the reasons why a longer period is required,

  II. the information that is required to complete the consultation, and

        III.   the estimated date on which consultation will be completed; or

    ii.   if the consultation period proposed to be agreed to will end 150 or more days after the date on which consultation was initiated, obtains the consent of the applicant to such period.

The Secretary and the Federal agency may mutually agree to extend a consultation period established under the preceding sentence if the Secretary, before the close of such period, obtains the consent of the applicant to the extension.

2. Consultation under subsection (a)(3) shall be concluded within such period as is agreeable to the Secretary, the Federal agency, and the applicant concerned.

3.

    A. Promptly after conclusion of consultation under paragraph (2) or (3) of subsection (a), the Secretary shall provide to the Federal agency and the applicant, if any, a written statement setting forth the Secretary's opinion, and a summary of the information on which the opinion is based, detailing how the agency action affects the species or its critical habitat. If jeopardy or adverse modification is found, the Secretary shall suggest those reasonable and prudent alternatives which he believes would not violate subsection (a)(2) and can be taken by the Federal agency or applicant in implementing the agency action.

    B. Consultation under subsection (a)(3), and an opinion issued by the Secretary incident to such consultation, regarding an agency action shall be treated respectively as a consultation under subsection (a)(2), and as an opinion issued after consultation under such subsection, regarding that action if the Secretary reviews the action before it is commenced by the Federal agency and finds, and notifies such agency, that no significant changes have been made with respect to the action and that no significant change has occurred regarding the information used during the initial consultation.

4. If after consultation under subsection (a)(2), the Secretary concludes that—

    A. the agency action will not violate such subsection, or offers reasonable and prudent alternatives which the Secretary believes would not violate such subsection;

    B. the taking of an endangered species or a threatened species incidental to the agency action will not violate such subsection; and

C. if an endangered species or threatened species of a marine mammal is involved, the taking is authorized pursuant to section 101(a)(5) of the Marine Mammal Protection Act of 1972; the Secretary shall provide the Federal agency and the applicant concerned, if any, with a written statement that—

    i. specifies the impact of such incidental taking on the species,

    ii. specifies those reasonable and prudent measures that the Secretary considers necessary or appropriate to minimize such impact,

    iii. in the case of marine mammals, specifies those measures that are necessary to comply with section 101(a)(5) of the Marine Mammal Protection Act of 1972 with regard to such taking, and

    iv. sets forth the terms and conditions (including, but not limited to, reporting requirements) that must be complied with by the Federal agency or applicant (if any), or both, to implement the measures specified under clauses (ii) and (iii).

c. BIOLOGICAL ASSESSMENT.

1. To facilitate compliance with the requirements of subsection (a)(2), each Federal agency shall, with respect to any agency action of such agency for which no contract for construction has been entered into and for which no construction has begun on the date of enactment of the Endangered Species Act Amendments of 1978, request of the Secretary information whether any species which is listed or proposed to be listed may be present in the area of such proposed action. If the Secretary advises, based on the best scientific and commercial data available, that such species may be present, such agency shall conduct a biological assessment for the purpose of identifying any endangered species or threatened species which is likely to be affected by such action. Such assessment shall be completed within 180 days after the date on which initiated (or within such other period as is mutually agreed to by the Secretary and such agency, except that if a permit or license applicant is involved, the 180-day period may not be extended unless such agency provides the applicant, before the close of such period, with a written statement setting forth the estimated length of the proposed extension and the reasons therefor) and, before any contract for construction is entered into and before construction is begun with respect to such action. Such assessment may be undertaken as part of a Federal agency's compliance with the requirements of section 102 of the National Environmental Policy Act of 1969 (42 U.S.C. 4332).

2. Any person who may wish to apply for an exemption under subsection (g) of this section for that action may conduct a biological assessment to identify any endangered species or threatened species which is likely to be affected by such action. Any such biological assessment must, however, be conducted in cooperation with the Secretary and under the supervision of the appropriate Federal agency.

d. LIMITATION ON COMMITMENT OF RESOURCES.—After initiation of consultation required under subsection (a)(2), the Federal agency and the permit or license applicant shall not make any irreversible or irretrievable commitment of resources with respect to the agency action which has the effect of foreclosing the formulation or implementation of any reasonable and prudent alternative measures which would not violate subsection (a)(2).

e.

1. ESTABLISHMENT OF COMMITTEE.—There is established a committee to be known as the Endangered Species Committee (hereinafter in this section referred to as the "Committee").

2. The Committee shall review any application submitted to it pursuant to this section and determine in accordance with subsection (h) of this section whether or not to grant an exemption from the requirements of subsection (a)(2) of this section for the action set forth in such application.

3. The Committee shall be composed of seven members as follows:
   A. The Secretary of Agriculture.
   B. The Secretary of the Army.
   C. The Chairman of the Council of Economic Advisors.
   D. The Administrator of the Environmental Protection Agency.
   E. The Secretary of the Interior.
   F. The Administrator of the National Oceanic and Atmospheric Administration.
   G. The President, after consideration of any recommendations received pursuant to subsection (g)(2)(B) shall appoint one individual from each affected State, as determined by the Secretary, to be a member of the Committee for the consideration of the application for exemption for an agency action with respect to which such recommendations are made, not later than 30 days after an application is submitted pursuant to this section.

4.

   A. Members of the Committee shall receive no additional pay on account of their service on the Committee.
   B. While away from their homes or regular places of business in the performance of services for the Committee, members of the Committee shall be allowed travel expenses,

including per diem in lieu of subsistence, in the same manner as persons employed intermittently in the Government service are allowed expenses under section 5703 of title 5 of the United States Code.

5.

    A. Five members of the Committee or their representatives shall constitute a quorum for the transaction of any function of the Committee, except that, in no case shall any representative be considered in determining the existence of a quorum for the transaction of any function of the Committee if that function involves a vote by the Committee on any matter before the Committee.

    B. The Secretary of the Interior shall be the Chairman of the Committee.

    C. The Committee shall meet at the call of the Chairman or five of its members.

    D. All meetings and records of the Committee shall be open to the public.

6. Upon request of the Committee, the head of any Federal agency is authorized to detail, on a nonreimbursable basis, any of the personnel of such agency to the Committee to assist it in carrying out its duties under this section.

7.

    A. The Committee may for the purpose of carrying out its duties under this section hold such hearings, sit and act at such times and places, take such testimony, and receive such evidence, as the Committee deems advisable.

    B. When so authorized by the Committee, any member or agent of the Committee may take any action which the Committee is authorized to take by this paragraph.

    C. Subject to the Privacy Act, the Committee may secure directly from any Federal agency information necessary to enable it to carry out its duties under this section. Upon request of the Chairman of the Committee, the head of such Federal agency shall furnish such information to the Committee.

    D. The Committee may use the United States mails in the same manner and upon the same conditions as a Federal agency.

    E. The Administrator of General Services shall provide to the Committee on a reimbursable basis such administrative support services as the Committee may request.

8. In carrying out its duties under this section, the Committee may promulgate and amend such rules, regulations, and procedures, and issue and amend such orders as it deems necessary.

9. For the purpose of obtaining information necessary for the consideration of an application for an exemption under this section the Committee may issue subpoenas for the attendance and testimony of witnesses and the production of relevant papers, books, and documents.
10. In no case shall any representative, including a representative of a member designated pursuant to paragraph (3)(G) of this subsection, be eligible to cast a vote on behalf of any member.

f. REGULATIONS.—Not later than 90 days after the date of enactment of the Endangered Species Act Amendments of 1978, the Secretary shall promulgate regulations which set forth the form and manner in which applications for exemption shall be submitted to the Secretary and the information to be contained in such applications. Such regulations shall require that information submitted in an application by the head of any Federal agency with respect to any agency action include, but not be limited to—

1. a description of the consultation process carried out pursuant to subsection (a)(2) of this section between the head of the Federal agency and the Secretary; and
2. a statement describing why such action cannot be altered or modified to conform with the requirements of subsection (a)(2) of this section.

g. APPLICATION FOR EXEMPTION AND REPORT TO THE COMMITTEE.

1. A Federal agency, the Governor of the State in which an agency action will occur, if any, or a permit or license applicant may apply to the Secretary for an exemption for an agency action of such agency if, after consultation under subsection (a)(2), the Secretary's opinion under subsection (b) indicates that the agency action would violate subsection (a)(2). An application for an exemption shall be considered initially by the Secretary in the manner provided for in this subsection, and shall be considered by the Committee for a final determination under subsection (h) after a report is made pursuant to paragraph (5). The applicant for an exemption shall be referred to as the "exemption applicant" in this section.
2.

    A. An exemption applicant shall submit a written application to the Secretary, in a form prescribed under subsection (f), not later than 90 days after the completion of the consultation process; except that, in the case of any agency action involving a permit or license applicant, such application shall be submitted not later than 90 days after the date on which the Federal agency concerned takes final agency action with respect to the issuance of the permit or license. For purposes of the preceding sentence, the term "final agency action" means (i) a disposition by an agency with respect to the issuance of a permit or license that is subject to administrative review, whether or not such disposition is subject to judicial review; or (ii) if administrative review is sought with respect to such disposition, the decision resulting after such review. Such application shall set forth the reasons why the exemption applicant considers that the agency action meets the requirements for an exemption under this subsection.

    B. Upon receipt of an application for exemption for an agency action under paragraph (1), the Secretary shall promptly (i) notify the Governor of each affected State, if any, as determined by the Secretary, and request the Governors so notified to recommend individuals to be appointed to the Endangered Species Committee for consideration of such application; and (ii) publish notice of receipt of the application in the Federal Register, including a summary of the information contained in the application and a description of the agency action with respect to which the application for exemption has been filed.

3. The Secretary shall within 20 days after the receipt of an application for exemption, or within such other period of time as is mutually agreeable to the exemption applicant and the Secretary

    A. determine that the Federal agency concerned and the exemption applicant have

        i. carried out the consultation responsibilities described in subsection (a) in good faith and made a reasonable and responsible effort to develop and fairly consider modifications or reasonable and prudent alternatives to the proposed agency action which would not violate subsection (a)(2);

        ii. conducted any biological assessment required by subsection (c); and

        iii. to the extent determinable within the time provided herein, refrained from making any irreversible or irretrievable commitment of resources prohibited by subsection (d); or

    B. deny the application for exemption because the Federal agency concerned or the exemption applicant have not met the requirements set forth in subparagraph (A)(i), (ii), and (iii). The denial of an application under subparagraph (B) shall be considered final agency action for purposes of chapter 7 of title 5, United States Code.

4. If the Secretary determines that the Federal agency concerned and the exemption applicant have met the requirements set forth in paragraph (3)(A)(i), (ii), and (iii) he shall, in consultation with the

Members of the Committee, hold a hearing on the application for exemption in accordance with sections 554, 555, and 556 (other than subsection (b)(1) and (2) thereof) of title 5, United States Code, and prepare the report to be submitted pursuant to paragraph (5).

5. Within 140 days after making the determinations under paragraph (3) or within such other period of time as is mutually agreeable to the exemption applicant and the Secretary, the Secretary shall submit to the Committee a report discussing
    A. the availability of reasonable and prudent alternatives to the agency action, and the nature and extent of the benefits of the agency action and of alternative courses of action consistent with conserving the species or the critical habitat;
    B. a summary of the evidence concerning whether or not the agency action is in the public interest and is of national or regional significance;
    C. appropriate reasonable mitigation and enhancement measures which should be considered by the Committee; and whether the Federal agency concerned and the exemption applicant refrained from making any irreversible or irretrievable commitment of resources prohibited by subsection (d).
6. To the extent practicable within the time required for action under subsection (g) of this section, and except to the extent inconsistent with the requirements of this section, the consideration of any application for an exemption under this section and the conduct of any hearing under this subsection shall be in accordance with sections 554, 555, and 556 (other than subsection (b)(3) of section 556) of title 5, United States Code.
7. Upon request of the Secretary, the head of any Federal agency is authorized to detail, on a nonreimbursable basis, any of the personnel of such agency to the Secretary to assist him in carrying out his duties under this section.
8. All meetings and records resulting from activities pursuant to this subsection shall be open to the public.

h. EXEMPTION.
1. The Committee shall make a final determination whether or not to grant an exemption within 30 days after receiving the report of the Secretary pursuant to subsection (g)(5). The Committee shall grant an exemption from the requirements of subsection (a)(2) for an agency action if, by a vote of not less than five of its members voting in person—
    A. it determines on the record, based on the report of the Secretary, the record of the hearing held under subsection

(g)(4) and on such other testimony or evidence as it may receive, that—

    i.   there are no reasonable and prudent alternatives to the agency action;

    ii.   the benefits of such action clearly outweigh the benefits of alternative courses of action consistent with conserving the species or its critical habitat, and such action is in the public interest;

    iii.   the action is of regional or national significance; and

    iv.   neither the Federal agency concerned nor the exemption applicant made any irreversible or irretrievable commitment of resources prohibited by subsection (d); and

B. it establishes such reasonable mitigation and enhancement measures, including, but not limited to, live propagation, transplantation, and habitat acquisition and improvement, as are necessary and appropriate to minimize the adverse effects of the agency action upon the endangered species, threatened species, or critical habitat concerned.

Any final determination by the Committee under this subsection shall be considered final agency action for purposes of chapter 7 of title 5 of the United States Code.

2.

A. Except as provided in subparagraph (B), an exemption for an agency action granted under paragraph (1) shall constitute a permanent exemption with respect to all endangered or threatened species for the purposes of completing such agency action

    i.   regardless whether the species was identified in the biological assessment; and

    ii.   only if a biological assessment has been conducted under subsection (c) with respect to such agency action.

B. An exemption shall be permanent under subparagraph (A) unless—

    i.   the Secretary finds, based on the best scientific and commercial data available, that such exemption would result in the extinction of a species that was not the subject of consultation under subsection (a)(2) or was not identified in any biological assessment conducted under subsection (c), and

ii.   the Committee determines within 60 days after the date of the Secretary's finding that the exemption should not be permanent.

If the Secretary makes a finding described in clause (i), the Committee shall meet with respect to the matter within 30 days after the date of the finding.

i. REVIEW BY SECRETARY OF STATE.—Notwithstanding any other provision of this Act, the Committee shall be prohibited from considering for exemption any application made to it, if the Secretary of State, after a review of the proposed agency action and its potential implications, and after hearing, certifies, in writing, to the Committee within 60 days of any application made under this section that the granting of any such exemption and the carrying out of such action would be in violation of an international treaty obligation or other international obligation of the United States. The Secretary of State shall, at the time of such certification, publish a copy thereof in the Federal Register.

j. Notwithstanding any other provision of this Act, the Committee shall grant an exemption for any agency action if the Secretary of Defense finds that such exemption is necessary for reasons of national security.

k. SPECIAL PROVISIONS.—An exemption decision by the Committee under this section shall not be a major Federal action for purposes of the National Environmental Policy Act of 1969 (42 U.S.C. 4321 et seq.): *Provided,* That an environmental impact statement which discusses the impacts upon endangered species or threatened species or their critical habitats shall have been previously prepared with respect to any agency action exempted by such order.

l. COMMITTEE ORDERS.

   1. If the Committee determines under subsection (h) that an exemption should be granted with respect to any agency action, the Committee shall issue an order granting the exemption and specifying the mitigation and enhancement measures established pursuant to subsection (h) which shall be carried out and paid for by the exemption applicant in implementing the agency action. All necessary mitigation and enhancement measures shall be authorized prior to the implementing of the agency action and funded concurrently with all other project features.

   2. The applicant receiving such exemption shall include the costs of such mitigation and enhancement measures within the overall costs of continuing the proposed action. Notwithstanding the preceding sentence the costs of such measures shall not be treated as project costs for the purpose of computing benefit-cost or other ratios for the proposed action. Any applicant may request the Secretary to carry out such mitigation and enhancement measures. The costs incurred by the Secretary in carrying out any such measures shall

be paid by the applicant receiving the exemption. No later than one year after the granting of an exemption, the exemption applicant shall submit to the Council on Environmental Quality a report describing its compliance with the mitigation and enhancement measures prescribed by this section. Such a report shall be submitted annually until all such mitigation and enhancement measures have been completed. Notice of the public availability of such reports shall be published in the Federal Register by the Council on Environmental Quality.

m. NOTICE.—The 60-day notice requirement of section 11(g) of this Act shall not apply with respect to review of any final determination of the Committee under subsection (h) of this section granting an exemption from the requirements of subsection (a)(2) of this section.

n. JUDICIAL REVIEW.—Any person, as defined by section 3(13) of this Act, may obtain judicial review, under chapter 7 of title 5 of the United States Code, of any decision of the Endangered Species Committee under subsection (h) in the United States Court of Appeals for (1) any circuit wherein the agency action concerned will be, or is being, carried out, or (2) in any case in which the agency action will be, or is being, carried out outside of any circuit, the District of Columbia, by filing in such court within 90 days after the date of issuance of the decision, a written petition for review. A copy of such petition shall be transmitted by the clerk of the court to the Committee and the Committee shall file in the court the record in the proceeding, as provided in section 2112, of title 28, United States Code. Attorneys designated by the Endangered Species Committee may appear for, and represent the Committee in any action for review under this subsection.

o. Notwithstanding sections 4(d) and 9(a)(1)(B) and (C), sections 101 and 102 of the Marine Mammal Protection Act of 1972, or any regulation promulgated to implement any such section—

   1. any action for which an exemption is granted under subsection (h) shall not be considered to be a taking of any endangered species or threatened species with respect to any activity which is necessary to carry out such action; and

   2. any taking that is in compliance with the terms and conditions specified in a written statement provided under subsection (b)(4)(iv) shall not be considered to be a prohibited taking of the species concerned.

p. EXEMPTIONS IN PRESIDENTIALLY DECLARED DISASTER AREAS.—In any area which has been declared by the President to be a major disaster area under the Disaster Relief and Emergency Assistance Act, the President is authorized to make the determinations required by subsections (g) and (h) of this section for any project for the repair or replacement of a public facility substantially as it existed prior to the disaster under section 405 or 406 of the Disaster Relief and Emergency Assistance Act, and which the President determines (1) is necessary to prevent the recurrence of such a natural disaster and to reduce the potential loss of human life, and (2) to involve an emergency situation which does not allow the ordinary procedures of this section to be followed. Notwithstanding any other provision of this section, the Committee shall accept the determinations of the President under this subsection.

Endangered Species Act (ESA) Triggers

Most types of FEMA-funded projects have the potential to trigger the ESA. Projects with the highest likelihood of impact include:

- New construction.
- Work in water.
- Debris operations.

When the ESA is triggered, consultation with U.S. Fish and Wildlife Service (USFWS) or the National Marine Fisheries Service (NMFS) (also known as NOAA Fisheries) may be required. These consultations should be completed by subject-matter experts and can take months. An accurate project description is key to expediting the process.

ESA: Streamlining Tools

FEMA has negotiated various agreements that simplify and expedite the ESA review process. These agreements address routine activities with minimal potential to affect listed species and critical habitat.

The agreements allow FEMA to approve certain types of projects without extensive USFWS/NMFS consultation. A good scope of work is needed to determine whether projects fit under these agreements.

Select this link to view the Memorandum of Agreement between FEMA and U.S. Fish and Wildlife Service (Tennessee/Kentucky Field Office) and the Kentucy Department of Fish and Wildlife Resources.

Protecting an Endangered Species

Dr. Mike Forstner:
The Houston toad is actually a unique individual amphibian species. In Texas, it not only occurs in very few counties and Bastrop actually happens to be the largest population

prior to the fire. It was the last place that it was doing well. The largest population in Bastrop County has been impacted by 40 percent of the habitat changed in the fire.

Ronnie Moore:
This fire was not only one of the most horrific fires in Bastrop County's history, this was the most horrific fire in the state of Texas' history. In Bastrop County we had of 38,000 acres burned, over 1,600 residential structures burned, totally burned to the ground, and we had 2 fatalities, 2 losses of life. It was a horrific disaster.

Slate:
Sept. 9, 2011: Major Federal disaster declared for Bastrop County amid the worst wildfires in state history. Clearing the way for FEMA recovery assistance to Texas wildfire survivors and their communities

Kevin Hannes:
The Houston Toad is a rare species that is on the endangered species list. We have both the toad that's an endangered species, that's trying to recover from the fire, and we have our citizens of the State of Texas. They live together and so we want them to recover together to ensure that we have continuity of not only our survivors but also of the Houston Toad. Because FEMA is providing funding for the recovery in Bastrop, under the Endangered Species Act we are required by law to ensure that we protect the environment of an endangered species, in this case the Houston Toad. We only had two options: one was to stop work completely during the chorusing season while the toad was active. That was not a viable option. Or we could agree to find a way to protect the toad while we continued the work. We brought in specifically trained wildlife biologists who are permitted and trained to handle the Houston Toad. So, if we locate a Houston Toad we can put them in a safe location so they can continue to recover and survive and we can continue this recovery process for the citizens of Bastrop.

Kevin Jaynes:
January 10, we brought all the parties together, all the agencies: Parks and Wildlife, Fish and Wildlife, FEMA, of course, and developed the informal consultation strategy. It was a huge collaborative effort to make sure everyone was on the same page and that we could continue the work to get the survivors back into their homes and also maintain the habitat for the Houston Toad.

Ronnie Moore:
We are working together really in the spirit of cooperation between all the agencies. And it's great team work, really. Everyone leaves their egos and titles at the door, we step in, and it's just like the musketeers said, "All for one and one for all."

Dorothy Weir:
Not only do these toad monitors that FEMA's brought on have specific permits issued by US Fish and Wildlife to handle, identify, and relocate Houston Toads in the wild, they also really are the top experts in the field and, collectively, the team has over a century of experience dealing with the Houston toad in the wild and dealing in Houston toad habitat.

Melissa Jones:
They usually typically breed January to May, really kind of peaking February, March, April. They are going to find shelter in some of this leaf litter over night. We got pretty warm last night so there could have been some movement so what we wanted to make sure is that, before they had a pile to place all their debris they are cutting, that there wasn't a toad underneath that debris pile.

Amanda Aurora:
With the private property debris removal sites, we work with the cut crew and the debris removal crews to clear areas of the Houston toad. We show up at a property, we look at the trees that are numbered and try to figure out what the best ways are to bring them down. And then, where the trees might fall or where the equipment might run, we look through all the cover on the ground — leaf litter, logs, debris piles — and make sure there aren't any Houston toads under there that would get squished or run over by that equipment or the falling trees.

Dr. Mike Forstner:
The citizens of Bastrop County pride themselves on a rural lifestyle with rural values. It's really synergistic to maintaining that lifestyle to support the Houston Toad. The reason they moved to Bastrop County is because it looks a certain way. Maintaining that look maintains the habitat for the Houston Toad. And if we are able to do those two things, toads and people will continue to recover in the county.

Slate:
Recovery for the whole community Driving citizen recovery forward while protecting a rare native Texan that is also a wildfire survivor: the Houston Toad.

Kevin Hannes:
One of the things that's important to understand about this process is that it is working. Our toad monitors the other day came across a site and we located a female toad that was a juvenile and we were able to relocate it to its natural habitat here in Bastrop, so it can continue its recovery process in a safe environment away from the debris, away from the construction — so that we can continue to have the survivors of Bastrop recover as well as this rare endangered species, the Houston Toad.

Fish and Wildlife Coordination Act

Congress enacted this law to protect fish and wildlife affected by significant direct Federal actions that control or modify water bodies such as dams, reservoirs, harbor modifications, etc.

This act rarely applies to FEMA actions.

Migratory Bird Treaty Act

The Migratory Bird Treaty Act (MBTA):

- Makes it unlawful to pursue, hunt, take, capture, kill, or sell migratory birds.
- Protects migratory bird species, their nests, and eggs.

The U.S. Fish and Wildlife Service (USFWS) is responsible for enforcing this law, and the applicant is responsible for compliance.

Bald and Golden Eagle Protection Act

The Bald and Golden Eagle Protection Act provides additional legal protection for bald eagles and golden eagles which are also covered under the Migratory Bird Treaty Act. Bald eagles were delisted from the Federal list of threatened and endangered species in 2007.

FEMA activities that may trigger the Bald and Golden Eagle Protection Act include:

- Construction of communications towers.
- Clearing forested areas.
- Projects involving wetlands or coastal areas.

The U.S. Fish and Wildlife Service (USFWS) is responsible for enforcing this law, and the applicant is responsible for compliance.

Magnuson-Stevens Fishery Conservation and Management Act

The Magnuson-Stevens Fishery Conservation and Management Act protects fisheries of commercial interest, specifically "Essential Fish Habitat" (areas used "for spawning, breeding, feeding, and growth to maturity").

FEMA activities that may trigger this law include projects involving:

- Rivers.
- Estuaries.
- Coastal areas.

Consultation with USFWS and/or the National Marine Fisheries Service (NMFS) may be required.

Executive Order 13112: Invasive Species

Executive Order 13112 prohibits Federal agencies from funding actions that introduce or spread invasive species (non-native plants and animals). Examples of invasive species include:

- Emerald ash borer.
- Kudzu.
- Pythons.

FEMA activities that may trigger this Executive Order include:

- Vegetative debris removal and disposal.
- Vegetative erosion control measures.
- Wildfire fuel reduction grants.

Water Resources Laws

This lesson covers the resources laws and Executive Orders shown below.

- EO11988: Floodplain Management
- EO11990: Protection of Wetlands
- Clean Water Act
- Wild and Scenic Rivers Act

It is important to note that FEMA-funded actions in or near water often trigger a higher level of EHP review.

E.O. 11988: Floodplain Management and E.O. 11990: Protection of Wetlands

Executive Orders 11988 and 11990 grant protection to floodplains and wetlands because of their critical role in providing wildlife habitat, pollution control, and flood control.

E.O. 11988: Floodplain Management

Floodplain management is an important issue for FEMA because:

- Flooding is a major cause of disaster damage.
- FEMA administers the National Flood Insurance Program (NFIP) and publishes Flood Insurance Rate Maps (FIRMs).

The goals of E.O. 11988 are to:

- Maintain natural and beneficial floodplain values.
- Avoid development or new construction in floodplains.
- Evaluate potential effects of federal actions in floodplains.

In some cases, special requirements must be met before an action located in the floodplain can be funded (elevation, flood proofing, etc.).

What is a Floodplain?

A floodplain is . . .

Any land area susceptible to being inundated by floodwaters (e.g., areas adjacent to streams, rivers, coastal and tidal areas, urban runoff areas, and other low-lying areas).

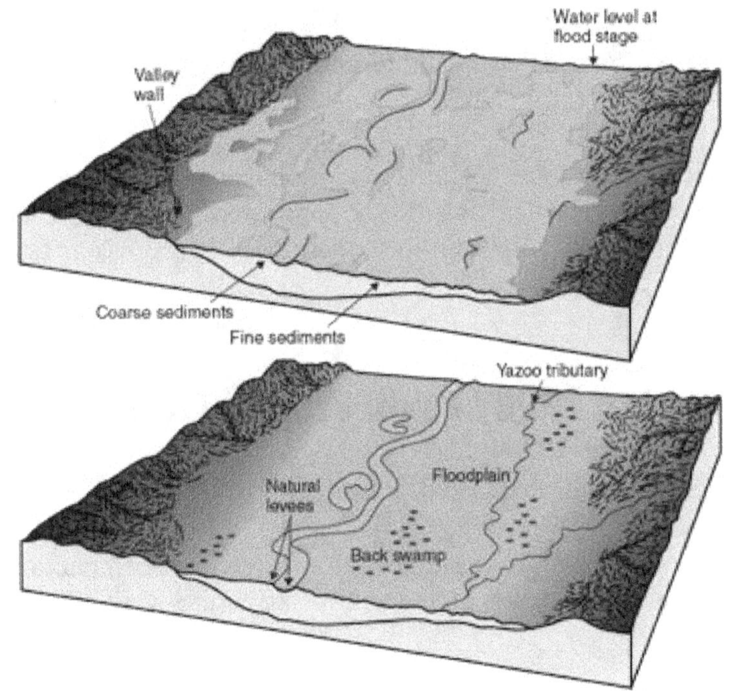

Floodplain Identification

Flood hazard areas identified on Flood Insurance Rate Maps (FIRMs) are identified as Special Flood Hazard Areas (SFHAs). SFHAs are defined as areas that will be inundated by the flood event having a 1-percent chance of being equaled or exceeded in any given year. The 1-percent annual flood chance is also referred to as the base flood or 100-year flood. SFHAs are designated on FIRMs as zones. Flood zones are defined by type, depth, and frequency of flooding.

- **Zones A/AE:** Areas subject to inundation by the 1-percent annual-chance flood event are generally determined using approximate methodologies. Zone A is subdivided into additional zones based on location and risk.
- **V-Zones/VE:**

FEMA actions in zones A or V are significantly restricted. Actions (e.g., elevation, flood proofing) cannot be funded without adherence to all restrictions.

Moderate flood hazard areas, labeled Zone B or Zone X (shaded) are the areas between the limits of the base flood and the 0.2-percent-annual-chance (or 500-year) flood and are also shown on the FIRM.

Zone X is identified by the following:

- Areas outside the flood zone are designated as Zone X and are unshaded on FIRMs.
- Areas that would be inundated by a 500-year flood (0.2-percent chance of flooding in any given year) appear as shaded areas on FIRMs.

Generally, areas designated as Zone X have little potential for FEMA EHP actions. **However,** critical actions (restoration of hospitals, EOCs, fire stations, etc.) are significantly restricted in shaded Zone X (500-year floodplain) areas.

E.O. 11990: Protection of Wetlands

Executive Order 11990, Protection of Wetlands, requires Federal agency actions to:

- Avoid, to the extent possible, adverse impact on wetlands.
- Avoid supporting actions affecting wetlands.

What Is a Wetland?

A wetland is an area of land in which the soil is saturated with moisture— either permanently or seasonally—and includes specific types of vegetation, soil, and hydrology. Specialists can identify wetlands on the basis of these features. Many natural and manmade environments can be classified as wetlands. Examples of wetlands include:

- Swamps.
- Bogs.
- Marshes.
- Bayous.
- Estuaries.
- Tidal areas.

Wetlands may be salt water, fresh water, or brackish—natural or manmade.

Wetlands and FEMA Actions

FEMA-funded projects in or near wetlands may require coordination with multiple agencies (i.e., U.S. Army Corps of Engineers, Environmental Protection Agency, State water-quality agencies).

Any action located in or near wetlands can incur additional costs, and alternatives should be identified, if possible.

Floodplains/Wetlands EOs: Eight-Step Planning Process

FEMA documents its decisionmaking for EOs 11988 and 11990 by completing an 8-step process. This process ensures that FEMA considers how its actions affect floodplains and/or wetlands.

Step 1, Determine Proposed Action Location: Determine whether the proposed action is located in a wetland and/or a 100-year floodplain (500-year floodplain for critical actions) and whether it has the potential to affect or be affected by a floodplain or wetland (see 44 CFR §9.7).

Step 2, Early Public Notice: Notify the public at the earliest possible time of the intent to carry out an action in a floodplain or wetland. Involve the affected and interested public in the decisionmaking process (see 44 CFR §9.8).

Step 3, Identify Alternative Actions: Identify and evaluate practical alternatives to locating the proposed action in a floodplain or wetland. Alternatives may include alternative sites or actions, as well as the "no action" option (see 44 CFR §9.9). If a practical alternative exists outside the floodplain or wetland, FEMA must locate the action at the alternative site.

Step 4, Identify Impacts: Identify the potential direct and indirect impacts associated with the occupancy or modification of floodplains and wetlands as well as the potential direct and indirect support of floodplain and wetland development that could result from the proposed action (see 44 CFR §9.10).

Step 5, Minimize Adverse Impacts: Minimize the potential adverse impacts and support to or within floodplains and wetlands to be identified under Step 4. Restore and preserve the natural and beneficial values served by floodplains, and preserve and enhance the natural and beneficial values served by wetlands (see 44 CFR §9.11).

Step 6, Re-evaluate Alternatives: Re-evaluate the proposed action to determine if it is still practical in light of its exposure to flood hazards, the extent to which it will aggravate the hazards to others, and its potential to disrupt floodplain and wetland values. Re-evaluate if alternatives preliminarily rejected at Step 3 are practicable in light of the information gained in Steps 4 and 5. FEMA shall not act in a floodplain or wetland unless it is the only practical location (see 44 CFR §9.9).

Step 7, Final Public Notice: Prepare and provide the public with a finding and explanation of any final decision that the floodplain or wetland is the only practical alternative (see 44 CFR §9.12).

Step 8, Implement the Action: Review the implementation and post-implementation phases of the proposed action to ensure that the requirements stated in 44 CFR §9.11 are implemented fully. Oversight responsibility shall be integrated into existing processes.

Clean Water Act

The Clean Water Act (CWA) is intended to restore and maintain the quality of the Nation's water resources by limiting pollution. To comply with the CWA, FEMA activities involving work in rivers, wetlands, estuaries, or other "waters of the United States" may require review and compliance under this law. Typical project types include:

- Culvert replacement.
- Bridge repair.
- Drainage improvements.
- Embankment restoration.

CWA Permits

Under the CWA, the U.S. Army Corps of Engineers (USACE) and State water-quality agencies issue permits, and the applicant is responsible for compliance. There are two types of permits.

- Individual Permits are required for larger projects with potentially significant impacts.
- General Permits are issued on a nationwide, regional, or State basis for specific categories of activities.

Applicants must coordinate with USACE and State agencies to obtain the appropriate permits before beginning work in water.

Wild and Scenic Rivers Act

The Wild and Scenic Rivers Act was created to preserve certain rivers with outstanding natural, cultural, and recreational values.

This act applies to all actions that affect rivers designated to have outstanding natural, cultural, and recreational values.

This law prohibits Federal agencies from undertaking activities which would adversely affect the values for which the river was designated.

Coastal Laws

Two prominent coastal laws also are applicable to FEMA projects:

- Coastal Barrier Resources Act (CBRA)
- Coastal Zone Management Act (CZMA)

Coastal Barrier Resources Act

The CBRA protects ecologically sensitive and geologically vulnerable barrier islands along the East Coast, Gulf Coast, and Great Lakes.

The CBRA is administered by the Department of the Interior through the USFWS.

CBRA restrictions only apply to Federal expenditures.

CBRA: Purpose

The purpose of CBRA is to:

- Prevent loss of life.
- Protect natural resources.
- Prevent wasteful federal expenditures.

To discourage development, the law prohibits the following in CBRA zones.

- Federal flood/disaster insurance coverage
- New Federal expenditures, including financial assistance for development

Coastal Zone Management Act

The Coastal Zone Management Act (CZMA) was passed in 1972 to preserve, protect, develop, and, where possible, restore and enhance resources in coastal zones.

The CZMA is administered by the National Oceanic and Atmospheric Administration (NOAA).

Most coastal areas, Great Lakes States, and territories have agencies that oversee compliance with the CZMA.

CZMA: Goal

The goal of the CZMA is to reduce uncontrolled coastal development by ensuring that Federal activities in the coastal zone are consistent with each State's Coastal Zone Management Plan.

The CZMA applies to any Federal action affecting land, water use, or natural resources of the coastal zone.

Pollution Control Laws

Several pollution control laws also affect FEMA programs.

- Clean Air Act (CAA)
- Resource Conservation and Recovery Act (RCRA)
- Comprehensive Environmental Response, Compensation, and Liability Act (CERCLA)

Most of these laws are managed by the States authority delegated by a Federal agency, generally the Environmental Protection Agency (EPA).

FEMA is responsible for ensuring applicants comply with these laws.

Clean Air Act

The Clean Air Act (CAA) sets limits on air pollutant emissions.

The CAA applies to FEMA actions, such as:

- Burning debris.
- Demolition of structures.

Compliance with CAA may require permits from State and local environmental agencies.

Resource Conservation and Recovery Act (RCRA)

This act establishes requirements for management of solid and hazardous wastes.

RCRA applies to FEMA actions that involve debris removal, staging, reduction, and disposal and is generally regulated at State and local levels.

To expedite review, it is important to report the location of staging areas, air curtain burners, and final disposal sites accurately.

RCRA: Application and Compliance

To comply with RCRA:

- Debris must not be staged in a wetland nor affect natural and cultural resources or public safety.
- Staging areas cannot become permanent disposal sites.
- Debris must be segregated and disposed in approved sites only.

Comprehensive Environmental Response, Compensation, and Liability Act (CERCLA)

CERCLA is a law that applies to large, complex contaminated sites (i.e., Superfund Sites) that may require extensive cleanup and site remediation.

CERCLA applies to FEMA actions, such as selection of temporary housing sites and facility relocations.

The EPA has the authority to coordinate cleanup of Superfund Sites.

Socioeconomic Laws

Two important socioeconomic laws affect FEMA actions:

- Farmland Protection Policy Act (FPPA)
- EO 12898: Environmental Justice in Minority Populations and Low-Income Populations

Farmland Protection Policy Act

The FPPA requires Federal agencies to examine potential effects before approving activities that convert farmland to other uses.

Farmlands can include citrus groves, orchards, tree farms, and other areas designated as "prime and unique."

New construction is the FEMA action most likely to require compliance and coordination with Natural Resources Conservation Service (NRCS).

EO 12898: Environmental Justice in Minority and Low-Income Populations

EO 12898 requires Federal agencies to consider whether their actions would adversely and disproportionately affect minority or low-income populations.

FEMA actions that may trigger this EO:

- Siting of debris locations
- Siting of temporary housing
- Relocation of critical infrastructure (schools, fire stations)
- Large-scale acquisitions/demolitions

Lesson Summary

In this lesson, you have learned about key environmental laws and Executive Orders as they affect FEMA and other agency actions.

- Biological laws and Executive Orders
- Water resources laws
- Coastal laws
- Pollution control laws
- Socioeconomic laws

In the next lesson, you will learn about FEMA's role in historic preservation.

Lesson 4: The National Historic Preservation Act

Lesson Overview

This lesson introduces the National Historic Preservation Act.

At the end of this lesson, you should be able to:

- Describe FEMA's responsibilities under NHPA.
- Identify potential historic properties.
- Identify FEMA actions that trigger historic preservation review.
- Discuss methods to expedite FEMA's historic preservation review process.

National Historic Preservation Act

The primary historic preservation law for the Nation is the National Historic Preservation Act (NHPA), which was passed in 1966. The NHPA:

- Established the basic framework for the practice of historic preservation.
- Assigned historic preservation responsibilities to Federal agencies.

The NHPA states that it shall be the policy of the Federal Government to "provide leadership in the preservation of prehistoric and historic resources of the United States."

NHPA Oversight Mechanisms

The NHPA established:

- The **National Register of Historic Places** (National Register) maintains an inventory the Nation's historic properties.
- The **Advisory Council on Historic Preservation** (ACHP) advises the President and Congress on matters of historic preservation and provides guidance to Federal agencies.
- **State Historic Preservation Officers** (SHPOs) administer State historic preservation programs.
- **Tribal Historic Preservation Officers** (THPOs): administer tribal historic preservation programs.

Section 106 of the NHPA

Section 106 mandates that Federal agencies will, prior to the approval of any expenditure of any funds, "take into account the effect of the [project] undertaking on any district, site, building, structure, or object that is included in or eligible for inclusion in the National Register."

What is a Historic Property?

As defined in the NHPA, a historic property is one that is listed in or eligible for listing in the National Register. To be listed in or eligible for listing in the National Register, a property must be:

- One of five defined resource types (i.e., building, structure, object, site, or district).
- Typically more than 50 years old.
- Significant within its historic context.
- One that retains its integrity such that it can convey its significance.

Defining Historic Properties

FEMA is responsible for identifying not only those properties that are currently listed on the National Register but also those that are eligible for listing.

All identification and evaluation of historic properties must be conducted by a qualified professional who meets the Secretary of the Interior's Professional Qualification Standards.

Archeology And Historic Preservation:
Secretary of the Interior's Standards and Guidelines
[As Amended and Annotated]

Professional Qualifications Standards

The following requirements are those used by the National Park Service, and have been previously published in the Code of Federal Regulations, 36 CFR Part 61. The qualifications define minimum education and experience required to perform identification, evaluation, registration, and treatment activities. In some cases, additional areas or levels of expertise may be needed, depending on the complexity of the task and the nature of the historic properties involved. In the following definitions, 1 year of full-time professional experience need not consist of a continuous year of full-time work but may be made up of discontinuous periods of full-time or part-time work adding up to the equivalent of a year of full-time experience.

History

The minimum professional qualifications in history are a graduate degree in history or closely related field; or a bachelor's degree in history or closely related field plus one of the following:

1. At least 2 years of full-time experience in research, writing, teaching, interpretation, or other demonstrable professional activity with an academic institution, historic organization or agency, museum, or other professional institution; or
2. Substantial contribution through research and publication to the body of scholarly knowledge in the field of history.

Archeology

The minimum professional qualifications in archeology are a graduate degree in archeology, anthropology, or closely related field plus:

1. At least one year of full-time professional experience or equivalent specialized training in archeological research, administration or management;
2. At least 4 months of supervised field and analytic experience in general North American archeology, and
3. Demonstrated ability to carry research to completion.

In addition to these minimum qualifications, a professional in prehistoric archeology shall have at least
1 year of full-time professional experience at a supervisory level in the study of archeological resources of the prehistoric period. A professional in historic archeology shall have at least 1 year of full-time professional experience at a supervisory level in the study of archeological resources of the historic period.

Architectural History

The minimum professional qualifications in architectural history are a graduate degree in architectural history, art history, historic preservation, or closely related field, with coursework in American architectural history, or a bachelor's degree in architectural history, art history, historic preservation or closely related field plus one of the following:

1. At least 2 years of full-time experience in research, writing, or teaching in American architectural history or restoration architecture with an academic institution, historical organization or agency, museum, or other professional institution; or
2. Substantial contribution through research and publication to the body of scholarly knowledge in the field of American architectural history.

Architecture

The minimum professional qualifications in architecture are a professional degree in architecture plus at least 2 years of full-time experience in architecture; or a State license to practice architecture.

Historic Architecture

The minimum professional qualifications in historic architecture are a professional degree in architecture or a State license to practice architecture, plus one of the following:

1. At least 1 year of graduate study in architectural preservation, American architectural history, preservation planning, or closely related field; or
2. At least 1 year of full-time professional experience on historic preservation projects.

Such graduate study or experience shall include detailed investigations of historic structures, preparation of historic structures research reports, and preparation of plans and specifications for preservation projects.

National Register of Historic Places

The National Register of Historic Places:

- Is the official inventory of historic properties in the United States.

- Includes historic properties that are significant at the local, State, national, and tribal levels.
- Is maintained by the National Park Service (NPS).
- Contains more than 85,000 listings of buildings, sites, structures, objects, and districts.

National Register Resource Type: Building

The National Register defines a "building" as a resource that "is created principally to shelter any form of human activity." Examples include:

- Churches.
- Schools.
- Courthouses.
- Barns.
- Country stores.
- Gas stations.
- Motels.
- Shotgun houses.
- Suburban tract houses.

Chrysler Building, New York, NY. Designed by William Van Alen, completed in 1930 and listed in the National Register in 1976 (at 46 years old). A soaring example of the Art Deco, it was briefly the tallest structure in the world. It is also a National Historic Landmark.

National Register Resource Type: Building

Buildings do not have to be large, elaborate, or highly-ornamented to be eligible for listing. Historic buildings can be ordinary in appearance and associated with the everyday lives of people.

Workers' housing such as this was designed by the mining companies to provide housing for miners and other workers. U.S. Coal and Coke Company established the Gary Works, 12 individual company towns in McDowell County, WV.

National Register Resource Type: Structure

The National Register defines a "structure" as a resource that is made "for purposes other than creating human shelter." Examples include:

- Aircraft.
- Automobiles.
- Boats.
- Bridges.
- Canals.
- Culverts.
- Dams.
- Grain elevators.
- Highways.

Completed in 1883, the Brooklyn Bridge is one of the oldest suspension bridges in the U.S. John Augustus Roebling designed the structure to connect Manhattan with the bustling borough of Brooklyn. It was one of the first structures to use caissons during construction, and is a National Historic Civil Engineering Landmark. It was listed in the National Register in 1966 and is also a National Historic Landmark.

National Register Resource Type: Object

The National Register defines "objects" as resources that are "primarily artistic in nature or are relatively small in scale and simply constructed." Objects must be associated with a specific setting or environment to be eligible for listing in the National Register. Examples of objects include:

- Boundary markers.
- Fountains.
- Mileposts.
- Monuments.
- Sculptures.
- Statuary.

Built in 1937, the statues of Paul Bunyan and his companion, Babe the Blue Ox, are among the most famous status of the folk hero and ax man. The display was added to the National Register in 1988.

National Register Resource Type: Site

The National Register defines "site" as a resource that "is the location of a significant event, a prehistoric or historic occupation or activity, or a building or structure, whether standing, ruined, or vanished, where the location itself passes historic, cultural, or archaeological value, regardless of the value of any existing structure." Examples of sites include:

- Battlefields.
- Campsites.
- Ceremonial sites.
- Ruins of buildings or structures.
- Shipwrecks.

Archaeological resources are generally categorized as sites. Resources with prehistoric/historic religious and/or cultural significance to Native Americans are often categorized as sites.

Among the best-known landmarks on campus are the two Indian mounds. It is believed the mounds are over 5,000 years old and date back to before the construction of the great Egyptian pyramids. In the 1980s, scientists from the LSU Museum of Natural Science, the Department of Agronomy, and the Department of Geography & Anthropology collected soil samples from the bases of the mounds and discovered they were part of a group of Archaic mound complexes located throughout the State. In 1999, the Indian Mounds at LSU were listed on the National Register of Historic Places.

National Register Resource Type: District

The National Register defines a "district" as a "significant concentration, linkage, or continuity of sites, buildings, structures, or objects united historically or aesthetically by plan or physical development." Examples of districts include:

- Business districts.
- Canal systems.
- College campuses.
- Estates or farms.
- Residential neighborhoods.
- Rural villages.

Lowell Locks and Canals Historic District, Lowell, MA. One of the country's first true industrial cities, Lowell's prominence is largely due to its lock and canal system. Water power from the Merrimack River powered the prolific textile mills of the 19th century.

The district remains almost entirely intact, and was listed as a National Landmark District in 1977.

What are Some "Historic Property" Clues?

Some historic properties are marked by plaques or markers but not all are clearly marked. Some clues to identifying historic properties that indicate the necessity for additional followup include:

- Single buildings or concentrations of buildings that are clearly "old."
- Unusual architectural styles or design features.
- Groupings of properties with similar appearance or functions such as mills or farm buildings.
- Areas that seem to be a focal point for the community.
- Undisturbed land or known archaeological sites.

Any of these clues should be included in the project documentation or scope of work.

Section 106 Process

Section 106 is a process, not an outcome. To be in compliance with the law, a Federal agency must go through the Section 106 process. Throughout the process, the Federal agency retains decisionmaking authority.

The Section 106 Process Does . . .	The Section 106 Process Does Not . . .
<ul><li>Ensure that FEMA has considered the effects of its actions on historic properties.</li><li>Require consultation with the SHPO/THPO and other interested parties.</li></ul>	<ul><li>Require the preservation of historic properties.</li><li>Automatically stop a FEMA project from moving forward.</li></ul>

The Section 106 Process

The Section 106 process involves four steps, each of which is intended to answer a question about the project.

A. Establish the Undertaking, answers the question: **What are we doing?**
B. Identify and Evaluate the Undertaking, answers the question: **Are there historic properties in the area?**
C. Assess Adverse Effects, answers the question: **Will the project negatively impact historic properties?**
D. Resolve Adverse Effects, answers the question: **How can we offset the impact to historic properties?**

Section 106 Consultations and Determinations

It is FEMA's responsibility to determine what effect projects will have on historic properties.

These determinations are documented in consultations among FEMA, SHPO/THPO and other interested parties.

FEMA Actions That Trigger NHPA Review

Different project types have different potential levels of impact.

FEMA-funded actions with the greatest potential to impact historic properties include:

- Demolition.
- Renovation.
- Elevation.
- Modification.
- New Construction.
- Excavation.
- Relocation.

Implementing the Section 106 process

FEMA is required to complete the entire Section 106 process for each project. For projects with significant effects to historic properties, the consultation process can take months.

While FEMA is responsible for ensuring that treatment measures are implemented, who bears the responsibility for implementing the measures is determined on a project-by-project basis.

Streamlining the Section 106 Review

FEMA has negotiated programmatic agreements in many States that simplify and expedite the Section 106 process. These agreements outline the routine activities with minimal potential to affect historic properties.

Programmatic agreements allow FEMA to approve certain types of projects without extensive SHPO/THPO consultation. The use of programmatic agreements for Section 106 is similar in practice to the use of CATEXs under NEPA.

The use of programmatic agreements requires a well-defined scope of work.

Tribal Consultation Requirements

- Federally recognized Indian tribes are sovereign nations.
- The Federal Government interacts with tribes on a government-to-government basis.
- FEMA must ensure that tribes have a reasonable opportunity to participate in the Section 106 process.

The National Historic Preservation Act in Action

Cindi Hendrickson
In 2008, the city experienced a 500-year flood that devastated a lot of properties. 600 properties in the city were damaged. Over 300 of those needed to be demolished. One of those properties was a residential property that had been a former schoolhouse that was built in 1927, that was substantially damaged and could not be repaired. As part of FEMA's requirements to mitigate damages to historic properties, we needed to find a

project that we could use and direct some funding toward. What we did was solicit proposals from our local historic society and the Little Red Schoolhouse Museum popped up as, as just a, a perfect example of what we would wanna do.

Rita Congdon
Little Red Schoolhouse was a schoolhouse here in Black Hawk County and it was built in 1911. There were hundreds of one-room schoolhouses here in Iowa but by the mid-60s they had been phased out with consolidation. It was in very bad shape. It was in very bad shape. It desperately needed to be painted. Pieces of paint peeling off, you know, as big as my hand. And as the children would come up the back door on the ramp, when they would come in from recess you know, you see peeling paint there and you're a kid, what're ya going to do?

Cindi Hendrickson
What was done was siding replacement. There were several areas of rotting siding and to keep sympathetic repairs for the original, a lot of the siding was replaced and repainted.

Rita Congdon
The boardwalk. It was very splintery. And so they provided the material and one of our Kiwanis groups donated the labor. It was very much appreciated that we could get a professional painter and get a nice, get the nice siding. We have no more ugly boards or boards that you touch and they're soft.

Cindi Hendrickson
The Little Red Schoolhouse Museum is a hands-on, you know, the kids can go in there, and you know actually sit at the desks and, and you know, see what it was really like.

Rita Congdon
June 20th, 1911 and this is what (voice trails off) They started with a one-week class and then it started to grow and they added a second class, a second one, and I've seen it go from three, four, five and now this is our second year to have six, one-week sessions for children. We do the four Rs', readin', writin', rithmetic and recess. It is such fun because the kids who are here want to be.

Cindi Hendrickson
Since the repairs have been made it stands out. It's just kind of a shining little red schoolhouse now. It receives lots of visitors young and old lot of kids that get to go through that.

Rita Congdon
For a community that is interested in history it gives a very good idea of what, what things were like 100 years ago. And I think our community appreciates the past.

Lesson Summary

You have completed Lesson 4. You should be able to:

- List the different types of historic properties.
- State the types of FEMA projects that may affect historic properties.
- Identify streamlining techniques for the Section 106 process.

Lesson 5 will present a review of the key points of this course and prepare you to take the final exam.